The
PLIGHT
of the
RURAL CHURCH

Also in this series:

The McGeachy Papers Vol. I, *Toward a Justice that Heals*, Morton MacCallum-Paterson, 1988.

The
PLIGHT
of the
RURAL CHURCH

R. Alex Sim
The McGeachy Papers Volume II

THE UNITED CHURCH PUBLISHING HOUSE
1990

ISSN 0840-6847

Canadian Cataloguing in Publication Data:
Sim, R. Alex, 1911-
   The plight of the rural church

(The McGeachy papers; v. 2)
Includes bibliographical references.
ISBN 0-919000-74-6

1. Rural churches.   2. Rural churches - Canada.
3. Community life.   4. Sociology, Christian.
I. Title.   II. Series.

BV638.S55 1990   254'.24   C90-094322-X

The United Church Publishing House
85 St. Clair Ave. E.
Toronto, Ontario
M4T 1M8

Publisher: R. L. Naylor
Editor-in-Chief: Peter Gordon White
Editorial Assistant: Elizabeth Phinney
Book Design: Graphics & Print Production
Cover Illustration: Alex Hawley
Printed in Canada by: Thistle Printing

5 4 3 2 1   90 91 92 93 94

Dedication

To my parents, Robert Sim and Alice Findlay Aitken.
They never failed their church in Gap View, Saskatchewan, which also served as a school, or in Holstein,
Ontario. Their daily family prayers and scripture reading
nourished our family spiritually and intellectually.

Contents

Acknowledgements ix

About the Series x

Introduction to this Volume xii

I. A Preface and a Parable for the Perplexed 1

II. Rural Reality and the Church 9

III. Chances for Change: Models and Options 19

IV. A New Ministry in a Rural Mode 33

V. Epilogue..43

References 44

Acknowledgements

Grateful thanks is extended to the McGeachy Senior Scholarship Committee for this opportunity to explore the condition and potential of the rural church; to those who patiently read and commented on early drafts: Douglas Brydon, Neil Lackey, Sharon Menzies, George Penfold and Joyce Sasse; to Olga and Peter McKellar for their encouragement and critiques; to Bette Shippam for word processing; and finally, to Barbara Sim who once again shared the pain of creation, and provided wise editorial comments. Whatever shortcomings that remain in the text are my own responsibility.

About the Series

The McGeachy Papers are your introduction to the impressive work being done by The United Church of Canada's McGeachy Scholars. This is an enterprise which continues to yield rich insights for both the church and the wider community. *The Plight of the Rural Church* by Alex Sim is the second volume in the Series, following Morton Paterson's work, *Toward a Justice that Heals*.

The McGeachy Memorial Senior Scholarship is a product of wealth derived from the inventive imagination and hard work of William A. and Margaret H. McGeachy in southwestern Ontario agriculture in the early decades of the twentieth century. The McGeachys bequeathed a substantial trust to The United Church of Canada through which they hoped to make possible a significant contribution to church and society in Canada. Recipients of the Scholarships are expected to identify and study important questions for reflection, faith, and hope in our time; and to express, and enable others to express, a faith which can speak to the hearts and minds of people, providing a reasoned and persuasive advocacy of the Christian gospel and way of life as alternative to the dehumanization of persons and the destruction of community going on all around us today. No theme is more timely or more appropriate to both the heritage and aims of the Scholarships than the one dealt with in this volume.

Future volumes in the McGeachy Papers series will include such themes as end-time consciousness in a nuclear age, Christian ethics in a Canadian context, contemporary symbols for communicating the Gospel in the late twentieth century, Bible stories for children with a new focus on the images of women in these stories, relating Christian beliefs to moral decisions, and the historical and ethical background of United Church decisions on social issues. The hope that the McGeachy Scholars would exercise and encourage within the church a prophetic vision that would call the people of God to their roots in God's self-revelation in Jesus Christ and rekindle their mission of justice, peace and the integrity of creation will not go unfulfilled.

Richard Moffat,
General Secretary
Division of Ministry Personnel and Education
June, 1990

Introduction to this Volume

For years now, voices from and on behalf of the rural church have been urging the national structures of the United Church to pay more attention to its plight. In choosing Alex Sim to be one of its McGeachy Scholars, the Division of Ministry Personnel and Education sought to answer this urging in a significant way. In his major McGeachy work, *Land and Community*, Alex Sim, scholar, farmer, and active rural church member, brings his wealth of knowledge and experience to bear upon the consciousness of the reader. Here in Volume II of the McGeachy Papers, *The Plight of the Rural Church*, Sim repeats some of the themes of his larger work while pointing with fresh and provocative insight to the implications of that work for the life, ministry and mission of the rural church. He articulates in an extremely readable and engaging fashion his conviction that the rural church must take on a new role as a distinctive rural institution with rich gifts of its own to give, if it is not to fail its people, reject its prophetic mission, or ensure its further decline.

In his insistence on a "renewed emphasis on the spiritual content of rural living, and a vigorous statement of rural values," Sim speaks *for* rather than *to* rural people. He seeks to mobilize their strength rather than to simply articulate their oppression. He calls for action — a rural manifesto, more rural literature, songs, textbooks, videos, television specials and sermons, and new institutes of rural studies.

We are met here by one who celebrates the strength and independence of rural people but who will not acquiesce in or accept the neglect and lower status which those qualities have often meant. Rural people have something precious to give us and Sim is not about to let either rural folk or urbanites forget it.

Sim's work is full of hard analysis, clear, practical suggestions, and lively theological reflection on the nature of church and ministry. What he offers us is not so much a finished product as a potent stimulus to our own thinking and a prod to our own action. As such, Sim's work is an invaluable resource for all who live and minister in a rural context and also for those who don't but who need to understand anew how rich are the gifts of rural life as well as how deep its problems. In the last analysis, Sim's work is also a warning to us to seek the welfare of the rural community and of the rural church, for in that welfare we will find our own.

Richard Moffat

The McGeachy Papers

I. Preface and a Parable for the Perplexed

It should surprise no one to discover that the church in rural Canada is facing unusual problems. How could it be otherwise in a country whose unity, and indeed whose sovereignty, seems to be at risk, in a world that is skating on the edge of an abyss? We need go no further than today's news to read about war, crime, pollution, fraud, bankruptcy, drugs, inflation, famine, epidemics, persecution, repressive regimes, trade deficits and a fluctuating dollar. Those who dream of getting away from it all will experience a rude awakening if they decide to flee to the countryside. There is no hiding place out here. Yet it will be argued in these pages that we rural people can do something about the problems that assail us, and that the church, even while facing its own serious problems, can be an agent in community regeneration. In fact the crisis leaves the church no alternative. Not to act is to accept becoming impotent and irrelevant.[1]

These are perplexing times in which to plot a plan of action. Governments and big business rush from crisis to crisis. Learned experts disagree, each offering ponderous analyse and carefully hedged predictions. The denominations are struggling to resolve doctrinal differences and respond to noisy demands, many of which emanate from national political issues. Initiatives usually come from urban leaders and congregations which reflect their own preoccupations. If the denominational wagon has four wheels — city, town, suburban and rural — I would argue that the rural wheel gets the least grease because it seldom squeaks. This reticence runs deep in the rural tradition. It contains the strength of independence to which I intend to appeal when I ask the rural people to tackle their own problems. It also contains a weakness for it represents an acceptance of neglect and a lower status. The rural crisis has the church crisis within it while the church problems, in part at least, mirror the rural crisis. It is primarily our problem and we have to take the initiative but it requires a national and denominational responsibility as well. We all have reason to be perplexed and for those who are, I offer the parable of the hen for it illustrates my viewpoint. In fact it is drawn from my own experience as a farmer.

At one stage, my wife and I decided to expand our poultry operation. It was finally established after a good deal of effort and expense. Then our egg production began to decline. In something of a panic, I invited a very successful egg producer to look at our operation and, if possible, tell us what was wrong with our hens. He dropped in one day, looked around, sniffed the air, kicked up the litter, looked into the nests, handled the feed, and then, in the way of country people, he thought for a few minutes. Finally he turned to us with a question: "If you were a hen would you want to lay an egg in this place?"

Before his visit we knew we had a problem. Now we knew it was us. The plight of the hen was created by us and the improvements had to be made by us.

In these pages I present the plight of the rural church, as I see it, and as others have reported it to me. I go further. I suggest changes but since I have no real power to implement them, I go no further than to put to the reader a question similar to the one asked by our neighbour.

To Rural Members: Take a look at your congregational activities. Ask yourself: If I were a stranger moving into this community would I feel easy in the place? Would it be rewarding to become a member of this church?

To the Rural Clergy: Put yourself in the pew of one of your churches. Would you really want to keep coming back to participate in its activities, and to listen to your sermons?

To Teachers in Theological Colleges: If you were one of your students heading out to serve a rural church, would you feel adequately prepared?[2]

To Church Leaders: Is your denomination doing enough to justify the support you now receive from rural congregations?

To Those Outside the Church: Would you prefer to live in a country without organized religious activities?

The parable of the hen is based on a real life experience illustrating the dilemma of quantifying or counting eggs when the issue was the quality of the environment we were creating for the hens. Isn't it generally true that we try so often to quantify quality? We tend to use numbers to judge the vitality of an organization, attempting to satisfy the most profound needs of its members. There are too many efficiency experts in the church (and in the school system, too) that use the wrong yardstick. There are better ways to measure what is, in effect, the depth of a religious experience. We tend to make the same mistake when evaluating small congregations. A dozen people in an echoing auditorium cannot help but feel discouraged. But the group is not too small, the sanctuary is too big and too costly to maintain. Put the same group in a cosy living room before an open fire and the quality of the worship experience changes. We may say "small is beautiful" but we are still generally impressed by the size of buildings, fortunes, farms and budgets.

There are other criteria for weighing the effectiveness of congregational life and denominational leadership even if we cannot avoid counting attendance, dollars, voluntary work and the like. Although I do turn to statistics, I think I relied more heavily on observation and intuition in reaching my conclusions. My judgement, for whatever it is worth, is based on a lifetime of concern for the rural church. I have been active in rural church work as a local member. I have participated in workshops with rural clergy as far back as 1939 and my work as a community consultant has taken me to all 10 provinces, the Yukon and the eastern and western Arctic. This allowed me to attend religious services in countless small communities, as fellow worshipper and careful observer.

Still, what I have to say is only one person's opinion. Others may see things somewhat differently. There is no doubt my general statements will not fit every local situation. When decisions are made about closing down rural congregations, the principle criteria for weighing the effectiveness of congregational activities, and indeed of denominational leadership, seems to be numbers. Yet adding up such totals causes us to overlook many other important factors especially in the rural sector where the operations are on a smaller scale.[3]

The rural church is small. Its members are usually knit together by kinship and other such bonds. It has an informal method of reaching decisions that does not always require the formal machinery of committees and parliamentary procedure. There are positive qualities here that are overlooked if the ideal model of big urban churches, dimly lit cathedrals, or the mass rallies of evangelists are used as a measuring stick.

Last year my wife and I travelled extensively in Great Britain and the Continent. As we explored the mysterious treasures of the Sistine Chapel, Canterbury, and the Paisley Abbey where my great-grandparents were married, my mind kept going back to my first memory of church. I recalled summer meetings in the local school in southern Saskatchewan, with a group of hardy pioneers from Ontario, Norway, Aberdeen and Iowa squeezed into the immovable desks, the blinding prairie sun streaming through the big windows, my mother at the organ, and someone expounding the gospel behind the teacher's desk under a picture of Queen Victoria. There was no smell of incense, only of chalk dust, spilled ink, and carefully oiled floors. My memory tells me it was a genuine church. I must be forgiven for seeing religious search and spiritual experience as existing apart from a building or a budget or an eloquent sermon. If we can separate religious ends from ecclesiastical means our diagnosis of the problems of the rural church will be more fruitful. I resonate to the angry words of Amos, that ancient rural prophet, when he cried out:

> I hate and despise your feasts, and I take no delight in your solemn assemblies ... take away from me the noise of your songs; to the melody of your harps I will not listen. But let justice roll down like a river and righteousness like a mighty stream.[4]

I am examining problems but I do not wish to convey a negative picture. Despite neglect, or just possibly because of it, there is incalculable strength in the rural church. That sense of independence and integrity, that attachment to sanctuary and to a predictable order of service, that steadfastness and loyalty: such are the strengths of the rural church. Yet they are often impediments to the initiatives and flexible responses a changed community and a threatened environment demand.

Here is my summary of the main features to be considered in diagnosing problems of the rural church:

☞ The general decline in the vitality of community life has a negative influence on the organizations operating within it. In fact, the decline is interactive.

☞ There is a low level of consciousness of the uniqueness of rural living and the alienation of the rural sector from programmes and interests dominated by urban values and promoted by urban-based organizations.

▣ The high value rural people place on a church building stands in the way of exploring alternatives in liturgy and a more active form of participation in worship.

▣ The hierarchical structure of most national organizations, including religious ones, limits local control and discourages local creative developments.

▢ Shifting population: There is a continuation of outward movement of old-time residents, especially of their young people, and in some communities an inward movement of new residents, mostly retirees and commuters. Many congregations find it difficult to mix the new and the old.

☒ The model of placement of one or more clergy to one congregation results in almost every rural congregation realizing the part-time services of an ordained minister. Rural people seem reluctant to explore alternatives, as do the denominations and the theological colleges.

☒ Since rural church enrollments are usually small, they tend to be downgraded in a society where size is a value. This bias disfavours the smallest and weakest congregations.

☐ Theological colleges have been slow to recognize that urban candidates to the ministry need much more preparation for rural service.

☒ Low status of service in the rural ministry is an impediment to revitalizing the rural church.

This is the way I see the challenge assailing the rural church but I believe it can be met. As the parable made clear it is a challenge that each one of us must face up to as individuals, one that confronts each denomination, each theological training centre, and especially each rural congregation.

> *I see the rural community, not as a quiet haven to escape a turbulent world, but as a battered raft drifting downstream on a river of change. It hits a rock and part of it breaks off carrying away some of the occupants while those that remain grapple with other bits of debris in a frantic effort to reconstruct the raft. As others try to scramble aboard those already on board are undecided whether to welcome or cast them adrift.* (R. Alex Sim, *Land and Community: Crisis in Canada's Countryside*[5])

II. Rural Reality and the Church

 he reality in my community and yours is by no means an open book. Even there, among sights and sounds familiar to us, careful observation is required. The overall picture for rural Canada is even more obscure. Given the low level of interest and awareness of rural issues and the absence of sympathy for rural problems shown by scholars, policy makers and media commentators, it is easy to understand why rural reality presents such a cloudy image. Yet the problems of the rural church will not be brought into sharp focus without an acute awareness of the context within which the church struggles for relevance. Both local conditions and outside forces are at play. The village in the global village is not protected from the winds of change. It is no exaggeration to claim there is a rural crisis in which the church is caught along with the school, the post office services, fishery establishments and the family farm. Most of us need to open our eyes to the world we live in, so that we can understand our own situation better.

Let me illustrate from my own experience a view of the rural crisis and the plight of the rural church. One evening standing on the front steps of my farmhouse, I counted lights from 18 houses that had not been there when I bought my Ottawa Valley farm in 1955. Yet I had to admit I knew the names of only six of my "neighbours," and was on a borrowing/lending basis with only three of these. It occurred to me then that none of these recent arrivals had ever been seen in our friendly little white church by the side of the road. I suspect few, if any, had ever been invited. This place where I live is no longer a community, I told myself. The members of my church as a local branch of the Christian church had fallen down.

The loss of the close ties of neighbourhood is one feature of rural life today. Of course I knew the other farmers up and down the road, but we did not exchange work and we went to different churches. Many of the new people, mostly commuters, were virtual strangers. There was no welcome wagon when they moved in or sad farewell party when they moved out.

The Elusive Notion of Rurality

If Canada is an unknown country, as Bruce Hutchison claimed many years ago, the rural parts of the country are even more ignored and misunderstood. It has often been said that the WASPS run Canada despite the rhetoric about multiculturalism. I would go further. It is a WASPUM society — adding U for urban-centred and M for male-dominated. The word rural, when it is used at all, usually refers to farm people, less than four percent of the population, and their intractable problems. There is a tendency to ignore the rural non-farm population, an additional 20 percent or more (depending on the measure used) growing at about the same rate as the urban population.

I remember Pierre Elliott Trudeau raising a storm during the 1983 election campaign when he mused after driving at night through western Ontario's rich farmland:

> There was acre upon acre of farmland, and all we could see, though I placed my forehead against the

cold window, were little lights here and there. And I was wondering what kind of people lived in those houses, and what kind of people worked in this part of Canada, and lived and loved there.

The media took him to task for not knowing his constituency better, but no one undertook to inform him who these people are and how they live. The assumption that the whole society is urbanized is shared by sociologists and rural people themselves. A prairie farmer remarked to me, "We're all the same, city and country." My response was, "If what you say is true, it's a great pity. Surely there are some rural characteristics worth preserving even without turning back the clock."

It was disappointing to hear a fine, proud person shy away from the label "rural." Small town and village people have the same aversion. Paradoxically, many city people dream of finding a place in the country. Recently I read a learned paper about extensive population shifts from urban to rural... a recent trend. But the categories used were metropolitan and non-metropolitan. In the non-metropolitan class there were two types: adjacent and non-adjacent. Non-adjacent to what? A city, of course. What does it feel like to live in a non-metropolitan, non-adjacent place? Does it make young people proud of their rural background? Does such a negative label attract able young professionals to serve in a nameless milieu: clergy, nurses, teachers and social workers? Let us call ourselves rural and value our differences and distinctiveness from that which is urban.

Undoubtedly, the task of identifying what is rural is complicated. Increasing numbers of city people have moved to town and country. (In my view, centres of up to 10,000 should be classified as rural.) Commuters live in the country but work elsewhere, often in cities. Then, too, there are many types of rural community. In *Land and Community*, I identified four types to which I assigned descriptive fictional names: "Agraville," "Ribbonville," "Fairview," and "Mighthavebeenville."

Agraville is the aggressively growing administrative and commercial centre which serves an expanding hinterland. Its institutions, including its churches, benefit from the demise of smaller ones in the surrounding territory. Ribbonville is a small town surrounded by an influx of new residences, most of them strung along roadways linking it to large towns and cities. Many new residents are commuters. There is pressure on local congregations to expand and change, a source of possible new energy as well as tension and conflict. Fairview also attracts new people. There the resource is scenery. The land unsuitable for large scale farming is now occupied by new residents like weekenders and retired couples. Here again is a challenge to the church to accommodate to change. Mighthavebeenville is a place of declining numbers and dwindling resources. Here the church, if it has not already been closed, makes increasing demands on the faithful few.[6]

Except for Agraville, rural communities have been denuded of their institutions through the centralization and consolidation of services. This results in centralizing services in larger towns, and in housing them in larger structures. This removes personnel from the smaller centres with reduced payroll and a lower tax base. It also saps the vitality of community life, and in the process, bureaucrats assume more and more control of decision making. This process can be observed in the school, welfare agencies, the post office, and commercial outlets. Fortunately, the church lags behind in this trend so the church building is one of the few public places left in many rural centres. In addition to the heavy-handed decisions that close down services and reduce local autonomy there are other more subtle influences that have helped to transform rural life. These come through changes in the type of person living in towns and countryside, through television and consumerism, and through many other penetrating and complex factors. Meanwhile the rural church remains all too often a symbol of nostalgia and loss, and is seldom a forerunner and leader in the regeneration of rural society. But the edifice is still there. It stands, potentially at least, as a rebuke to a generation that is too busy scrambling after the dollar (often from necessity) to attend to matters of mind and spirit. The same forces that have destroyed the family farm and put the earth at risk are eroding community life and threatening the church. But until the rural church takes on a new role as a distinctive rural institution, it will have failed its people, rejected its prophetic mission, and ensured its own further decline.

The Rural Sector in One Denomination

My own study and intuition have led me to certain conclusions about the plight of the rural church. I have been able to find some support for these views from the excellent statistics provided by The United Church of Canada. Since I did not have the resources to canvass the other denominations, I recognize the dilemma of seeming to reach certain conclusions from the statistics of one denomination. I do not imply that they point to a general truth. I ask the skeptical reader to accept my generalizations as hypotheses which further research will undoubtedly modify and to which the unfolding future will provide its own inexorable answers.

The table below is drawn from a year end, 1988, statistical report. It shows the distribution of preaching places, pastoral charges and numbers of persons under pastoral care, between rural (centres under 2,000), towns (centres between 2,000-30,000), suburban centres (communities contiguous to cities), and cities (above 30,000). A pastoral charge is a unit of one or more preaching places administered by an official board representing each congregation and representatives of their organizations. Usually an ordained or diaconal person is employed to provide pastoral services.

The United Church of Canada
Statistical Report, December 31, 1988

	RURAL	TOWN	SUBURBAN	CITY	CANADA
Pastoral Charges	1,033	556	143	707	2,439
Preaching Places	2,366	865	168	737	4,136
Persons Under Pastoral Care	511,981	469,572	113,267	553,256	1.6m
Households under Pastoral Care	191,424	176,454	40,530	220,537	628,945

Membership Dec. 1988	243,757	228,406	60,048	312,877	845,088
Givers to Local Expenses	137,918	119,273	29,673	162,192	449,056
Givers to Missions & Service (i.e. to Headquarters)	63,205	65,187	18,631	104,272	251,295
Ave. Wkly Attend.	108,010	95,735	25,807	130,605	360,157
$ to HQ, incl. M&S	6.9m	8.4m	2.2m	14.8m	632.4m
$ per Charges	6,759	15,168	15,500	209,652	130,266
$ per Congregation	2,951	9,750	13,598	200,983	78,445
$ Raised for All Purposes	64.1m	66.3m	18.7m	122.3m	271.5m
$ Raised per Charge	61,983	119,306	131,125	173,044	111,756
$ Raised per Congregation	27,062	76,687	11,504	166,000	55,632

It is not unreasonable to compare rural and town totals with city and suburban. Town congregations do draw support from the surrounding countryside, and many of them have a second preaching point. If the two are combined there are 1,589 out of a Canadian total of 2,439 congregations outside of cities, while close to one million persons under pastoral care, out of 1.6 million, live in town and country.

Because of the great differences between regions in Canada, I give the breakdown by conference showing the percentage of persons under pastoral care in rural and town congregations. For Canada, 59 percent are found in rural and town settings with 41 percent found in city and suburban ones. The "trans-Canada" picture shows the following percentages coming from rural and town congregations: Newfoundland and Labrador, 84 percent; Maritimes, 74 percent; Montreal and Ottawa, 41 percent; Bay of Quinte, 73 percent; Toronto, 37 percent; Hamilton, 41 percent; London, 68 percent; Manitou, 68 percent; Manitoba and Northwestern Ontario, 61 percent; Saskatchewan, 72 percent; Alberta and Northwest, 68 percent; and British Columbia, 49 percent. The predominance of non-metropolitan numbers in most of Canada is remarkable. Even those conferences that use city names for the designations have large rural constituencies. Congregations in the Gaspé are in the Ottawa and Montreal Conference, while parts of Northern Ontario fall into the London Conference. As I have no way of knowing, I can only ask: Where do the power figures come from in these conferences? Who does most of the talking? In whose interest, rural or city, are decisions made?

In the rural column of the table we see over half a million people are claimed under pastoral care, about half of whom are members. In contrast to the half a million rural persons under pastoral care, only 180,010 on the average turn up for weekly service. This attendance is drawn from 191,424 households under pastoral care. "Givers" is another interesting category. Notice that the number of "givers" is much less than households. It should be recognized that in some households there may be more than one recorded giver. A total of 137,918 contribute to local expenses while less than half of this number, 63,205, direct their giving to the Mission and Service fund. One could conjecture that this latter group represents a hard core of those with strong identification with the larger enterprises of the denomination. It appears there are substantial numbers who are marginal or lukewarm toward those enterprises.

A close examination of data in the urban column will reveal that a higher proportion of those under pastoral care attend service, more money per giver is contributed, and a higher proportion pays into the Mission and Service fund. Rural people in the United Church send to headquarters $6,982,325, with grants coming back for various rural projects amounting to $1,453,560 a year, in addition to the general services provided by the national church which, in my view, are not particularly helpful. These figures suggest that apart from the greater wealth in cities available for giving, and perhaps easier access to the place of worship, that other factors, perhaps cultural or doctrinal, contribute to an apparent alienation of the rural sector from the denomination. The differences between rural and city data may also suggest financial strain is experienced by the rural congregations paying salaries and maintaining buildings. The spreading spore of rural poverty must not be discounted in all these calculations. It is possible too, that poor people feel more comfortable in rural congregations than in urban ones.

In conclusion, it appears that change is forcing the church to reassess its role and mission in the rural community. Yet the variety of community types will frustrate efforts to fashion uniform policies for the whole country. This circumstance suggests rural congregations must no longer wait passively to be rescued by new policies or pastors. Much better, let them become true pioneers fashioning their own revival. We can now explore possible solutions by outlining models and options for action and by presenting possibilities for a new type of ministry in a rural mode. It is hoped that the denominations will find ways to foster vigorous new initiatives at the local level.

The future has already broken into the present. We each live in many times. The present of one is the past of another, and the future of yet another. We are called to live knowing that the future exists, and that it is shared when it is lived. We cannot plan our way to humanity. Each one of us and each of the groups with which we live and work must become a model of the era we desire to create. The many models which will develop should give to each one of us an environment in which we can celebrate our creative response to change with others who need us. (Ivan Illich, The Church, Change and Development)

III. Chances for Change: Models and Options

lanning for change requires fundamental adjustments in outlook and commitment. Consequently, the plight of the rural church invites a rearrangement of denominational priorities. I find it difficult to reconcile the church's noble stand on justice for the weak and needy with policies that assign inexperienced and inadequately trained clergy to some of the most demanding and weakest pastoral charges in the country. I suggest the lay leadership of rural congregations could learn to be more assertive in church councils, while trying out new ideas and programs in their own congregations. Above all the uniqueness and beauty of small groups and small congregations should be asserted. Since every congregation has its own history, special conditions and precious hopes, it will be useful to examine these differences.

Some rural congregations suffer from loss of numbers. People either move out of the community or simply drop out of church life. Other congregations may lose numbers in the same way, even though new residents move into the community. If the newcomers enter into congregational life, there are problems of assimilation and of sharing leadership roles. If they stay away, the local congregation has problems such as those previously mentioned.

Where there are diminished numbers, the logical response is to close the church for economic reasons. The double cost of maintaining a church plant and paying part of a pastor's stipend, will dictate the decision to close. So a place of worship and the ordained leader are lost at one fell swoop. Perhaps only one of these supports needs to be lost. One or the other, building or clergy, might be retained. For instance, the building could be closed while the local group maintained its congregation life with all its intimacy and caring by moving the place of their meetings, if necessary, from house to house. The old church might be reopened at special times, or the group could join with others in suitable settings. By closing the building there might be sufficient resources for the congregation to claim and pay for pastoral services but the laity would need to intensify its "ministering" functions. The great Christian celebrations would be observed in some special way where large gatherings would enhance the sense of the occasion. The unseemly competition between denominations is a familiar complicating factor. Fortunately, necessity is rendering these attitudes obsolete. I now know of two congregations from different denominations using the same sanctuary and facilities at different hours on Sunday morning. In another case the two congregations in a small town meet together with the pastor from each denomination leading on alternate services. In this case the clergy are attached to seven or eight different congregations. Some congregations either skip services at regular intervals or meet without a pastor. Such strategies maintain congregational identity where population is dwindling.

Other communities are experiencing repopulation, with new people moving in. But the new and old do not always mix, at least not right away. The existing congregation could be energized by these new arrivals but for many reasons, more fully explored in *Land and Community*, this seldom happens. A whole new program of evangelism is needed to reach these new ruralites. I often hear hard-working church members complain that it is not a question of diminishing numbers at all, and that the churches would be full to overflowing if everyone would change their behaviour. I would like to hear more heart searching and less hand wringing. We need to ask ourselves (with genuine humility), why those who stay away do so.

Then there are strong rural congregations that face no immediate financial problems. Most of these are located in towns or prosperous villages. Such congregations may be experiencing other problems that spring from generational differences, or from disagreements in doctrine, or type of liturgy. Why is it that controversy and misunderstanding so often rise out of differences of faith? Sometimes a group chooses to withdraw in order to find another place of worship or a compromise is reached leaving both parties dissatisfied. I believe that a spirit of tolerance, surely one of the Christian virtues, should allow groups with strong differences to meet separately in the same building. When necessary each group could choose its own pastor.

To meet these various types of changed community we could consider several alternatives for congregational organization. The chief obstacle preventing consideration of these alternatives is the way we cling to tradition. Those of us who are older are especially prone to resist change. For instance, I still prefer the King James Bible. It may be reassuring to us in a confusing world to cling to old habits. But if young people and newcomers feel uncomfortable and excluded, and if we cannot change happily, let us maintain our own small group and encourage others to do likewise. The pioneers brought with them from Europe an ideal of an edifice with a sanctuary led by an ordained pastor whose constant requirement is the delivery of sermons. This model does not fit the contemporary rural scene. The energy required to raise money and maintain the property is excessive. It tends to distract from Bible study, meditation, prayerful self-examination and mutual support. This is why I stress worship and study in small groups, with a much more flexible system combining congregational resources with the utilization of the services of ordained personnel.[7]

Let us now examine a series of options that congregations and denominations could consider in coping with changes in our own lives and in society as a whole.

1. The Small Autonomous Group

The rigorous encouragement of small groups dedicated to worship, study, and fellowship will constitute a formidable challenge to the mainline denominations, since it is a strategy for service that runs counter to established practices. Moreover the selection and training of clergy with aptitude in pulpit appeal seems to run counter to those needed in a skillful and self-effacing group facilitator. I insert the word "autonomy" here to warn established congregations and denominations that this development will take place outside their structures unless they recognize its importance.

The Christian church began with a small group combined on occasion with mass gatherings. John Wesley's method was based on classes of 12, a practice still followed in some Methodist churches, even large urban ones. He also preached at mass rallies. We need both.

This option suggests a congregation can and should be capable of a meaningful religious experience without a church building, when too few people and too few dollars are available to keep it going.

Up to now, when a church was closed its members were expected to go elsewhere. Experience has shown that this transfer does not work very well. Significant numbers of adherents of closed churches quit going to church, or to put it more cruelly, they join their neighbours whose indifference or withdrawal had already weakened the congregation. Is it possible the energy expended in raising money and maintaining a building had turned its members into drudges suffering from burnout? They had become "Marthas" rather than "Marys." Let us look to the past for instruction.

Pioneer communities in Canada regularly began religious activity before they had a church edifice, even before they could attract a preacher. At that stage a ministry of self-help was at work. They sang without an organ and even without hymn books. Someone who knew the words said a line. It was then repeated as a response. Looking back at countless personal experiences in religious services, from urban cathedrals to small country churches, it is possible none were more devout or intimate than a worship fellowship around a campfire beside a lake, among close friends and with a trusted leader. Yes, I think we can worship without a building officially dedicated for that exclusive use.

I presume the "church" in Ephesus and Corinth met whether or not Paul was there on one of his infrequent visits. I presume they met in someone's house, or out of doors. But Paul, who was a brilliant letter-writer, kept in touch. We have great writers today too. We have the photocopier, the fax machine and other mechanical means of communication through which autonomous groups could be helped to study and worship. I recognize that there is still a yearning for a special place of worship among those churches who meet in schools and other such places. They continue to see such arrangements as an alternative rather than a preference.

Is it not possible we rural people today are over-dependent on having a church building, on having someone preach to us, or pray for us? Is it not possible that the demands put upon a small congregation to maintain a building and to pay a professional preacher may cut them off from a creative religious life? The efforts required become ends in themselves: the money to be raised; the arrangements; the committees; the denominational machinery; the agony of finding a minister that pleases everyone; the uncertainty of recruiting and holding an organist, Sunday school teachers, and a janitor. These demands are especially onerous in small congregations where numbers are diminishing and where young people are forced to move away to find jobs. In such situations the development of small groups is particularly appropriate.

On the other hand, many rural communities are gaining in population, but the new ruralites, for whatever reason, may not immediately join the local church. Yet they gradually lose contact with their church in the city, if in fact they ever had one. An alert liaison between urban and rural churches can help to bridge a gap. But where newcomers do not readily fit in, assuming that they would enjoy an opportunity to worship, and share their concerns about a spiritual life, perhaps a small group in the church or in the recreation room of a neighbour would fit their immediate needs.

Those deprived of regular church services in their community, through closure or for whatever reason, do have the option of those kitchen meetings that our ancestors chose. This option is also applicable to large urban congregations where it is hard to find regular intimate contact with like-minded searchers. I know in some urban settings, small groups meet in each others' homes to satisfy a hunger not answered by the fine music, the eloquent sermon, and the large impersonal crowd. We should not overlook this option in the country.

It is possible that the fostering of small autonomous groups and the development of a theological position that is in tune with rural values of neighbourhood and ecological responsibility may have to be pioneered by small groups outside existing congregations. This could be the necessary developmental phase before the new ideas percolate through the more rigid structures of our various denominations, and those local congregations that are sluggish about changing.

2. The House Church

As a nucleus of searchers for spiritual discovery and meaning becomes more solidly established, it may eventually acquire a permanent base where it can keep the books, materials and objects that add meaning to worship. Where numbers are few or where funds are limited there should be no eagerness to acquire property (and a mortgage). They should be praised for having chosen, like Mary, that good part. Ideally a series of such groups should be loosely connected with a mother congregation where they might draw support in theological instruction and in whose celebrations they might participate. On the other hand, if a network of such groups continued to prefer small group experience, they might combine to employ a full- or part-time professional leader or, alternatively, have one or more of their members receive instruction for a diaconal type of ministry. Or such groups might be connected electronically to a great teacher who, like Paul, would visit periodically.

3. The Saddlebag Preacher

There is a well-established tradition for an itinerant ministry. We need to find a modern model for continuing that tradition as a means of bringing new life and spirituality to the rural church especially for very small congregations and autonomous groups.

What is being proposed is an itinerant clergyperson who would move about the country sharing leadership with local lay leaders. Such a system might help to reduce dependency on a full-time professional preacher and a costly place to meet. In pioneer times, there was the saddlebag or circuit rider tradition. There are many other examples of itinerant ministries.

I recall the evangelists who visited our village periodically. The revival services would run for about a week. A service every night in one of the churches was well attended and generously supported financially. There was much gospel singing, often led by the evangelist's wife. I can recall anniversary services when a favourite pastor would be invited back. There were also the periodic visitations of missionaries from foreign fields which provided occasions of celebration, excitement and renewal.

I do not ignore the difficulties in establishing this type of fluid ministry within the rules and rigidities of the denominations. The yearnings of local congregations for a resident shepherd are against it as well. Nevertheless I can report several brave attempts to maintain such a ministry.

There are the sky pilots of the far north who in the bush pilot tradition visit scattered settlements to preach and administer the sacraments. There is the ship *Crosby* that voyages up and down the Pacific coast whose skipper is an ordained minister. There was an interesting program in Saskatchewan called the "Saddlebag Experiment" and the still functioning Northern Pastoral Region (NPR) in the Bay of Quinte Conference, Ontario.

In the Saddlebag Experiment an ordained person was appointed to work in an area where rapid depopulation had led to some church closures and to weakness and lethargy in many remaining parishes. The duties of this appointee included house to house visitation in helping people find and express their Christian faith. It did not include regular preaching except for special events of a festive nature. There was a strong support committee responsible for supervision, but, for reasons that are still rather obscure, funding for the experiment was withdrawn. Apparently those served by what appears to have been a popular ministry were unable to muster enough substantial financial support to sustain it.

The Bay of Quinte Conference of the United Church includes an area that fronts Lake Ontario with rich farmland and industrialized cities such as Oshawa, Kingston and Brockville. Behind this fringe is a large area, part of the Laurentian Shield, dotted with beautiful lakes and rivers, abandoned farms, and declining villages. The NPR, established in 1975 and still functioning, maintains two ordained clergy with special skills in group process and adult education who lead worship, meet church boards, do counselling, and fill in when vacancies occur.[8]

In recommending an itinerant ministry, a word of caution is in order. A model of intervention should be avoided where something is imposed from the outside. What is recommended is a response to genuinely felt aspirations. Paul's endeavours in Thessalonica and Athens (*Acts 17*) which seem to me to combine sensitive observation and fearless exposition, is an approach itinerant pastors could try to emulate. Paul, it must be remembered, was carrying on his trade as a tentmaker at the same time. Then the revival of a rural ministry could be accelerated and energized by the dedicated efforts of itinerant ministers, and would become fruitful.

4. Part Time Clergy

As already noted, almost all rural congregations are serviced by a part-time clergy in the sense that two or more congregations share the expense and benefits of a pastor. The positive and negative effects of this arrangement are well known. It has encouraged independence and autonomy in the congregations that have strong local leadership. But where this is lacking the result has been a declining and dispirited congregation. It so happens that the clergyperson, unless endowed with extraordinary energy, cannot invest the attention the weak congregation needs without neglecting the others. Only in exceptional cases does the strong congregation, which has been putting in the most dollars, help the weak by reducing its claims on the preacher by picking up the slack with increased lay involvement.

There should be a constant search for new solutions to the basic dilemma of almost every rural congregation: not enough dollars to employ a full-time parson. I should add that the present practice of assigning theological students to rural charges seems to be unfair and exploitative. The charges that cannot finance a full-time person have to accept what the denomination has to offer and thus, in a sense, contribute to that person's training. In city churches the novice works under the close supervision of a senior pastor with a much more limited range of responsibilities.[9]

Other types of part-time ministry come to mind. One is where an individual arranges two sources of income: one from the church, the other from a second job. Another is where one spouse, usually the wife, combines homemaking and the ministry while the major source of income is earned by the other spouse.

Today, when electronic connections, commuting, and other arrangements have allowed more professionals to live in the country and still pursue an outside career, it is possible that many rural communities could find a pastor among their own residents.

Dual or multiple careers can be very rewarding, provided burnout can be avoided. I can testify to this risk from my own experience, as can most women who have had to combine housekeeping and mothering with an outside job. It is important to see that part-time pay is matched by part-time work.

5. *Community Church*

A local congregation with no specific denominational flag is a common sight in company towns, especially those in prairie, northern, or isolated places, but is rare in most rural communities. Yet a community church is one way to keep the church doors open and the lights on if neighbours in the area can agree to ignore sectarian differences. I can report on such an experiment. I will call it Strawberry Hill. A well built and furnished church sits at the crossroads in a fertile valley devoted to mixed farming and cash crops, including strawberries. It had been a Baptist church but for many reasons the Baptist membership declined, leaving too few active members to meet its financial obligations. Finally it was offered for sale. The neighbourhood responded by saying, "No way, we want to keep a church and social centre among us."

The telephone lines began to hum, people talked about it when they met, meetings were held, resolutions passed. Finally money was subscribed to take over and maintain the old church. It now functions with broad support across the denominational front although some members keep in touch with their own denominations as well. Pastors are recruited in various ways. One was a retired minister, another a professional man with theological training. There is not sufficient revenue to engage a full-time pastor, and so the ministry is shared, as it should be, among its own members. There is a strong Sunday school. This congregation takes an active political stand on many issues. There is a lively interest in ecological programs. Support has been given to beleaguered groups in countries that suffer under a repressive regime. There are other examples of one denomination being dominant with adherents from other doctrines invited to give their support; hardly an ecumenical arrangement. In other places the pastor is drawn from each denomination alternatively with contributions directed to headquarters according to the choice of the donor.

6. Clustering[10]

If weak rural congregations and autonomous religious study groups are to thrive rather than merely survive, and if they are to receive superior, experienced leadership, new strategies must be found or invented. Our objective should be to enrich the experience within the small unit and to offer variety and stimulation to the members as well as to leaders and clergy. It is not surprising that we seek two opposing goals: to maintain the integrity of the isolated group or congregation and to break open that isolation with fresh initiatives and variety. Clustering, or cooperative arrangements between congregations and their leaders, lay and clergy, has been seen as one way of balancing these two forces.

There is nothing new about clustering. Consider, for instance, the three point charge, the team ministry, the larger parish. But it may be that a new name will encourage us to think of new variations on well-established themes. A cluster is an arrangement whereby two or more congregations undertake activities or projects together, whether informally, on a once-only basis, or formally, with legal and financial glue to ensure continuity. A cluster can be arranged between denominations on an ecumenical basis or within one denomination. We examine the cluster idea here to see how it can or has been utilized in revitalizing the rural church. In fact it may be the only way small congregations can secure the services (even if part time for each congregation) of a full-time, resident, ordained, pastor. In other cases it has been found more satisfactory to appoint lay or diaconal supply. This is less complicated and less expensive since fewer congregations have to be drawn together and satisfied.

A cluster can bring together congregations from one denomination in which case a rather wide territory would be encircled by the arrangement. Or congregations from several denominations can come together within a smaller circumference. Whatever the area covered, the arrangement is intended to provide a service that single congregations or charges with one clergy cannot manage by themselves.

The simplest type of cluster takes the form of a joint project like a vocation school, a day care centre, a seminar, or an evangelical event. These often occur in one community across denominational boundaries. Given the inherent rivalry that is often found between congregations, strong leadership is required for a program which is too demanding for one alone to undertake.

Larger enterprises call for formal and complex arrangements with the pooling of resources between congregations, and the sharing of responsibilities between the clergy. Clustering makes unusual demands as compared to the usual rural charge. It requires more planning and committee work, more travel, since an area served may be greatly enlarged — and more vision. It involves a surrender of a certain amount of congregational autonomy. It is also a challenge to the independence and freedom of congregational leadership as the egos of the clergy and lay leaders may be threatened. In short, inertia, self-interest, and tradition may stand in the way of innovation.

Despite these negatives, the advantages are impressive. A cluster brings together enough contributing families to assemble necessary resources. It allows for a fully equipped office, and the selection of clergy with training and aptitudes to serve specialized functions. Today, in denominations that permit the ordination of women, the husband and wife team who serve congregations shows promise. But the larger parish idea has not spread rapidly even though it seems to offer many advantages, and is favourably reported in the literature.

These models and options are only recommended for study and serious consideration. Each congregation considering change is urged to undertake careful self-study, and an honest appraisal of local strengths and weaknesses. It can be helpful to secure independent-minded consultation with experts who are sensitive to the advantages and obstacles involved in maintaining small congregations. What is at issue is finding optimal conditions for spiritual growth and responsible civic behaviour in your community. What is demanded? Work hard to analyse your situation, and humbly pray for grace, tolerance, and wisdom as you make your choices. Above all, do not stand in the way: give change a chance.

The Environment has a deep theological base and meets the Psalms with all the references to stewardship of the Earth and the limits of natural order. The moral dimension is often forgotten. (Jim Thompson, Bishop of Stepney, *The Guardian, 10.9.89*)

In preparing to deal with the current Canadian situation, we might well start by studying the classical doctrines of the theology of ministry and the theology of creation. That will give us a sound foundation upon which to build our prescription for the future of the practice of ministry, the search for justice, the stewardship of the earth, the yearning for the relevance of scripture in our complex times, an ethic for behaviour and action. (Sharon L.W. Menzies, *from a letter to the author*)

IV. A New Ministry in a Rural Mode

Having examined some of the options that could be considered for the rural church, I must confront other questions. How can the transformation of the rural church be brought about? Who is to lead this mission? How can we furnish the strong spiritual energy needed to refresh and drive this movement? The church can, should, and must, give leadership to this movement. As far as the church is concerned (collectively and within each denomination) we need *a new ministry in a rural mode.*

As we have a long way to go, it is time to get started. Our goal should not be limited to merely reviving ailing congregations but rather to spearheading a ruralization process which would counter the destructive aspects of urbanization and industrialization from which cities and Third World countries are as much victim as our own countryside. This calls for a new concept of ministry, a new emphasis on theological training, and a revised theology.

1. The Ministry Re-examined[11]

Having already looked at the usefulness of the church edifice, the role of the clergy should be examined — the second traditional pillar of the church program. In both cases, the difficulty of financing is linked to deeper questions of relevance and utility. No doubt there is still a need for church buildings and ordained persons but they could be utilized differently. For this reason I have avoided the word "minister" since it is so evident that ministering should be a widely shared responsibility.

Given the problems facing the rural church, ministry cannot be adequately provided, in the old way, by a salaried official. The old system that Charles Winters labels a "paternal" ministry is not working in rural churches or in small congregations generally. We need, Winters' argues, a widely shared "apostolic" ministry.[12]

The paternal model arose in the Middle Ages when one priest served one parish over a long period of time. His role justified the title of "father" for he was often the only educated person in the parish and he served as the leader in the mysteries of the sacraments, as confessor, as judge in disputes, and unquestioned arbitrator in the community. He came out of a community similar to the one he was chosen to serve. Over the years this role slowly changed as society changed, continuing to be reasonably satisfactory until recently. Today a rural congregation will most likely share its pastor with other congregations. The period of that person's tenure is usually brief, preparation for rural life inadequate, and expectations of the congregation regularly unrealistic. In all events the title of "father" or "mother" is much less appropriate than "brother" or "sister."

I have some knowledge of the hopes expressed by local congregations when searching for a new pastor, or seeking with varying degrees of subtlety to dispose of an unsatisfactory incumbent. They want a jack-of-all-skills who will, above all, lead an exemplary life but they expect to be disappointed. I have heard people say, "If we are lucky enough to call a really brilliant young pastor, he or she won't stay long." They have been rural people too long to be optimistic. Perhaps because there is a tendency for fatigue (there is a rat race in the country too) and burnout, there is a danger of leaning back and waiting for their incumbent to do much of the ministering they could do themselves.

There is reason to suggest that the tendency toward high specialization, observable in most professions, has made its impact on the orientation of the clergy as well. This trend, which is a response to the explosion of scholarly and scientific information, has rendered the ordinary citizen increasingly dependent upon experts.[13] In church work, the specialist in theology and religious education is in demand in urban situations while the rural pastor working alone must remain a generalist. This statement is from a rural pastor in western Canada:

> Even today in many rural villages that lack a doctor, lawyer, or local school, the minister remains the "educated" person in town and therefore is called upon for advice in all areas of life. We do law, medicine, social activism, intervention, finance, mental health counselling and much more because there is no one locally to fulfill these functions. For some this can be very intimidating. For me it has always proven to be the impetus to become better informed on issues that affect the lives of my people.

Here is another central problem for the rural church: the low status accorded service in rural parishes which reflects current attitudes toward rural clergy. This response is not entirely because of salary disparity and the lack of cultural stimulation when rural and urban careers are evaluated. Underlying it is the sense that rural work is out in the sticks or the boondocks. Another contributing factor is the diminishing number of candidates to the ministry who come from rural parishes with the resulting problem of adjustment to rural ways and small-scale operations.

In seeking to enhance the status of the rural clergy we should find a way to honour those who choose to devote their entire lives to rural work. If we could do so it would provide the young people entering the ministry with a needed role model. I notice, for instance, that in recent years the United Church has elected to its highest office two women, two lay persons and two representatives of visible minorities. A farmer, well known for his service as a layman, was defeated in the last election. Perhaps it is time to elect a rural pastor or lay person, not as a token of repentance for rural neglect, but as a signal for new policies.

If the church is to respond positively to the problems that beset it, a new type of ministry must be developed. New ways of deploying the theologically trained persons who are needed must be found. It is time to begin to think and work for an apostolic type of ministry as practised by Paul, Peter and the other apostles after Pentecost.[14]

2. A Rural Theology?
When I call for a rural theology, I am aware that there is a legitimate objection to such a proposal because of the danger of separating rural concerns from mainstream contemporary thought and scholarship. There is a fear that a demand for rural theology would further ghettoize the rural church, downgrading it still further in the church's priorities. For me "rural theology" is only a convenient label for a cluster of ideas that would help to make the

work of the church more relevant for rural people seeking goodness and justice in a confusing and frightening world. I am looking for religious activities, including sermons and teaching, that are appropriate in idiom and focus to the contemporary rural scene. Perhaps the title of this chapter is a better way of stating what is required. If theology is nothing more than a scholarly discipline concentrating on abstract, cerebral and philosophical questions, it is out of touch with the everyday anxieties and yearnings of ordinary people, including this writer. I will venture to suggest two points of emphasis for a rural theology, one having to do with the environment (relationship with nature), and the other having to do with neighbourhood (relationships with each other). I will state them as two propositions but in practice they are inseparable.

Rural congregations need clear teachings on biblical grounds on sensitive and responsible environmental questions. These should fearlessly guide and judge personal behaviour as well as commercial and governmental policy. An elemental step requires a new reading of Genesis: "he shall have dominion over...." If this injunction really means that he (and she) shall be responsible before God for the management and protection of the environment, I can see more people walking to the nearest church to worship, more people gardening as an alternative to golf and jogging, more farmers practicing a sustainable agriculture, and more money for research into methods of restoring and rebuilding that which we have thoughtlessly destroyed.[15]

A rural theology will need a return to the social gospel restated to confront current preoccupations with the acquisition of material things. There is a system of ideas in the world which is foreign to the sermon on the mount. Such ideas attempt to explain and justify increasing poverty and widespread starvation, the spread of militarism and racism, and the oppression of the weak and defense-less: children, women, visible minorities, the imprisoned, the mentally ill, and the legally disenfranchised. This ideology constitutes, in effect, an invisible religion in which people pin their faith on the machine (the chip is our latest icon), the infallibility of the scientist and the engineer, the beauty of gigantic buildings, the desirability of huge fortunes and big organizations, and the rightness of a personal narcissistic gratification.

A rural theology should speak to the world as it is today and still reaffirm old values: neighbourhood and community, caring for one other, sharing resources, smallness and intimacy, transcendence and spirit. Our best chance for survival is a revitalized Christian ethic of restoration and survival. The church would promote a program for the ruralization of our society to balance and correct the excesses of urbanization and industrialization. It is what the rural church has always stood for, but it should do so with more vigour and self-confidence.

3. A Program of Revival

Up to now I have been dealing in generalities, with the words "should" and "must" sprinkled generously throughout the text. But exhortation is not enough. A concrete program of action is essential. Ultimately many minds and lives must contribute so I value the opportunity to make my proposals here, gratefully anticipating the corrections and contributions of others. There are several critical questions that I cannot answer. How will the fire be lit? Who will put a match to the fuel? When will it occur? Recent history has been full of surprises where the people after years of oppression have said, "Enough." In many cases the church offers active opposition, often in the underground. It is true that the church has not been silent in this country on countless issues of exploitation and injustice including farm bankruptcies, plant closures and the depletion of natural resources. These are specific issues which should now be addressed. Here are some preliminary steps that could be taken in revitalizing religion in rural areas. In my view there should be renewed emphasis on the spiritual content of rural living, and a vigorous statement of rural values.[16]

4. Stages of Mobilization Envisaged [17]

Given the geography of Canada, the lack of funds available for national meetings, and the importance of involving as many denominations, regions, and points of view as possible, a loosely organized committee of correspondents could provide a modest beginning. One recalls the minutemen who brought the isolated American colonies together by mail or courier before and after the Boston Tea Party.

A few initial steps and some long-term goals are attainable by writing letters either in the old fashioned way or by modern electronic means. A few people concerned enough to begin to share ideas and make plans could begin to move mountains. No doubt funds will be needed. The Secretary of State, a foundation or two, and the denominations could be approached by an *ad hoc* group or by a sponsoring organization with sufficient neutrality to be accepted by the diverse interests of those involved.

A manifesto or a statement of goals would undoubtedly pass through several versions. A preliminary one would be needed to recruit members to the committee, and for use in seeking money and other resources. A number of statements are already on record dealing with the plight of the rural church. This essay is one of many. All could be drawn upon to stimulate debate resulting in a wider concensus, and (one would hope) even wiser conclusions.

The publication of a manifesto could rivet attention on rural issues, and create a growing awareness of the importance of rural people and the natural resources they live among and of which they are custodians. In addition to a manifesto, we need a rural literature: novels, poems, songs, textbooks, videos, television specials and sermons. I stress the importance of a literature because our knowledge of rural Canada is abysmally limited. To begin we need documentation about lively and imaginative innovative social arrangements, including church programs. There is much to which we can point with pride. Our lazy and self-depreciating Canadian habit of letting American, British and French writers define social reality for us is slowly disappearing. We can do more to urge it along. As for rural issues, we rural people have not begun to assert ourselves. We have hardly begun to inform ourselves about ourselves.

Ideally there should be a well-funded centre or institute to put direction into the activities called for in these pages. Such a centre would foster research, encourage publications of all kinds, and offer both academic and informal training. There are several such centres in the United States that flourish under denominational sponsorship. In England, the Arthur Rank Centre is a sterling example. Located near Coventry at the National Agricultural Centre, it is supported by several denominations. It serves as an adult education centre for lay and clergy persons, and as a powerhouse for generating new ideas and programs for rural congregations and their leaders in England. It also welcomes foreign visitors, many from Canada, including this writer, who are inspired by and somewhat envious of its program.

Yet such an institute would be difficult to realize in Canada given our regional diversity, the strong American pull, our denominational differences and the current indifference to rural reality.

Despite all obstacles I suspect the Canadian solution will be a unique combination of "make do" and compromise. One approach would be to combine a rural church training and research activity within existing program centres.

There is one school of rural planning in Canada. There are several schools of social work that specialize in preparing students for rural service. In law, medicine, public health, library work, and theology, only fleeting reference is made to work in a rural environment. There are professional schools offering training in adult education, or extension methods that might be involved. Some of these are at universities with agricultural faculties, some with theological schools. It is on problems such as these that a committee of correspondence should fasten its attention. Ideally, such an institute should be shared between denominations.

There could be an accompanying adjustment in the theological colleges. At the same time the fine retreat houses, now operated by almost all denominations, could increase their educational emphasis on a shared ministry for youth and adults drawn from rural congregations. Perhaps we can expect a slow but relentless movement in all segments of our national life that will place more emphasis on the uniqueness of rural work and place a higher value on the small enterprises, including our rural congregations.

V. Epilogue

he rural church is like a grain of mustard seed. It has a hard shell, is pungent to taste, and is colourful in the field even when unwanted and unappreciated. It is small but as the parable of Jesus suggests, it has a great potential for growth.

The parable, as reported by Mark, is a sermon exemplary in its brevity, simplicity and power. In the Revised Standard Version, it reads like this:

> The Kingdom of God is like a grain of mustard, which when sown upon the ground, is the smallest of all seeds on earth; yet when it is sown grows up and becomes the greatest of all the shrubs and puts forth large branches, so that the birds of the air can make nests in the shade.

We farmers know mustard as a cash crop or a weed, and as an essential ingredient in homemade sausage. My own experience reveals another aspect. After buying a farm in the Ottawa Valley, we decided to plow a meadow long used as a pasture. There was no sign of mustard, but once the field was cultivated and the land brought into good tilth, we were surprised to find the mustard plant with its brilliant yellow flower competing sturdily with a crop of oats. Apparently, the seed had lain dormant all those years in the patient earth awaiting friendly circumstances to permit it to germinate and spring back to life and reproduction. Rural Canada awaits just such a spiritual awakening.

References

1. As a counter to my general pessimism about the prospect of human survival, and the capability of Christian doctrine and its churches to give effective leadership, I have been encouraged by Eugen Rosenstock-Huessy, *The Christian Future or The Modern Mind Outrun* (New York: Harper & Row, 1946), and by Robert Bellah et al., *Habit of the Heart: Individualism and Commitment in American Life.*

2. Throughout this essay I tend to view theological training rather critically. Yet these views are not based on an in-depth study. Rather they reflect comments of recent graduates and members of local official church boards. In 1983, I sent a questionnaire to theological colleges in Canada asking about special preparation of their students for rural work. Those that replied indicated little or no special attention to rural culture.

3. There is an extensive literature extolling the small church and suggesting programs appropriate to its small scale and rural conditions. These are recommended: J.W. Carroll, ed., *Small Churches Are Beautiful* (New York: Harper & Row, 1977); C.S. Dudley & D.A. Walrath, *Developing Your Small Church's Potential* (Valley Forge, PA: Judson Press, 1988); D.A. Walrath, ed., *New Possibilities for Small Churches* (New York: Pilgrim Press, 1983).

4. Amos 5: 21-24, Revised Standard Version.

5. R. Alex Sim, *Land and Community: Crisis in Canada's Countryside* (Guelph: University of Guelph, 1988), p. 16. This book provides the frame of reference for conclusions presented in this essay.

6. This classification and the structural analysis outlined in the next paragraph are developed in greater detail in *Land and Community*.

7. The choices should be made by the congregation. A program of self-examination could be helped by a recent issue of the P.M.C. Magazine: "Redirecting and revitalizing the Rural Ministry today with a study guide for congregational groups," *The Practice of Ministry in Canada*, May, 1988. Available from Rural Books, 108 Glasgow St. N., Guelph, Ontario, N1H 4W3. $2.00 postpaid.

8. The evaluation of the Saddlebag Experiment is in the library of the Saskatchewan Conference of the United Church, 1805 Rae Street, Regina, SA, S4T 2E3, and possibly in some theological colleges. The Reverend Joyce Sasse was the director of this experiment. Information about the Northern Parish Prefect is available from the Bay of Quinte Conference Offices at 218 Barrie St., Kingston, Ontario.

9. Roy Oswald, *Crossing the Boundary* (Alban Institute, 1975). This book deals sensitively with the cultural shock experienced when crossing from seminary to parish. It marks the shift from where rewards are from intellectual agility and acumen to a situation where practical skills are demanded — interpersonal and group relations, organizational skills, counselling, evangelism and Christian education. "In seminary these skills are denigrated." p. 12.

10. See a 24-page pamphlet by A.C. Tennies, *Clustering, A Tool for Ministry* (The National Councils of Churches in Christ in the U.S.A., 475 Riverside Drive, New York,

N.Y. 10027, 1977); and, Peter McKellar, *Alternative Models for Ministry, Non Metropolitan Concerns* (The United Church of Canada, 1977). Inexplicably, this 38-page document is now out of print. I have found nothing more recent than 1977. Does this mean clustering has been abandoned, or a new label found for an old formula?

11. Anne Squire, *Envisioning Ministry* (Toronto: The United Church of Canada, 1985).

12. Charles Winters, "Being the Church: An Affirmation of Smallness." *PRAXIS*, Winter, 1977. New quarterly of the Hartford Seminary Foundation.

13. This trend was identified 40 years ago in a study of child rearing where the parental insecurity and polite intimidation of parents by school and psychological authorities was noted. Seeley, Sim & Loosely, "The Layman and the Expert: The Belief Market." *Crestwood Heights* (Toronto: University of Toronto Press, 1956).

14. Such redeployment will require the assumption of more ministering roles by the laity. See Vera Dozier, *The Authority of the Laity* (Alban Press, 1982). The laity is challenged by Dozier to accept a ministering role, claiming they have given up their authority, and allowed religion to become a fragment of our common life rather than a bond. The Bible is tragically misused, transforming the Gospel of love into a collection of rules.

15. L. Weber, et al., *Theology of the Land* (Collegeville, Minnesota: The Liturgical Press, 1987).

16. A short, inexpensive, but powerful, critique of our society governed by technological values is relevant to this proposition. Jacques Ellul, *Perspectives of Our Age* (Toronto: Canadian Broadcasting Corporation, 1981).

17. In February, 1990, a number of Canadians were invited to participate in a workshop on the rural church at Bangor Theological Seminary. A British delegate also attended along with Americans from the eastern seaboard. No doubt proceedings will be published. At any rate, inquiries should be directed to Douglas Walrath, teacher and author at the Seminary, Bangor, Maine 04401. A Canadian caucus met on this occasion at which proposals were made for action in Canada, several of them in harmony with the suggestions put forward here. Lester and Marion Settle who were in attendance, offered space for follow-up in their publication, *Rural Gleanings*, RR #1, Debert, Nova Scotia, B0M 1G0.

900407